Self-Esteem for Teen Boys

A Clear Guide to Building Confidence, Overcoming Doubts, and Thriving as Your True Self

John Iverson

Introduction

Hey you. Yes, you! I see you. You thought that you were invisible to the world, huh?

I know what feeling invisible is like because I was there myself.

In the not-too-distant past, I was the boy who often felt like I fell short in every way. I would see others in class show confidence that I could only dream of. They very easily raised their hands in class while I struggled with questioning whether my answer was right or wrong, even when I was certain that it was the right answer.

I watched as my peers easily made friends while I overthought every interaction. *Was I saying the right thing? Did I use the right word there? Do they find me boring? Do I need to raise my voice?* All these made for some very awkward conversations with others, and this only made me feel worse about myself.

This then led me to try to become someone that I am not, just so that I could fit in.

If the above sounds familiar, then you are in the right place. Throughout this book, I take you through some of the lessons I learned about being myself that I hope will also help you improve how you feel about yourself. I learned these lessons later in life, but you don't need to wait to become an adult to learn these.

I know you might be thinking, *'Oh, another long lecture on being myself and whatnot. I have heard it all before.'* But no. I am not here to lecture you on what you should or shouldn't do or what you must or mustn't do. Rather, it is a conversation aimed at slowly unraveling the hidden gem hiding beneath that exterior shell of self-consciousness.

Throughout your life, I know you have been wondering so much about yourself, asking yourself questions such as:

Why do I always feel as though I never measure up to others, no matter how hard I try?

Why do I feel as though there is something wrong with me, but I can't figure out what it is?

Why can't I speak to others or ask my crush out, like the other boys? Is there something wrong with me?

Is it normal to feel the way I am feeling about myself?

How can I stop feeling as though I am being judged and watched at every turn?

How do I deal with people around me who constantly make fun of me and put me down?

If these questions and others are keeping you up at night, this book is here to shine a light on what may be causing you to feel the way you feel and how you can change that by covering the following:

- Why you should not blame yourself for the way you feel and why it's not all your fault.

- How to build your self-awareness and introspection so that you can understand who you are and get to the root cause of why you feel the way you do.

- How to silence the critical voice inside your head and instead, build a voice of affirmation to help you through any challenge.

- Ways of turning your doubts into a source of strength and pride

- How to uncover hidden talents and gifts within you and how to use them to build your sense of identity and confidence.

- How to build strong relationships with friends, and family who will help you thrive.

- And so much more!

Without further ado, then, let us begin working on improving your self-esteem and making you more confident in facing the world ahead of you.

Table of Contents

Chapter 1: Shining a Spotlight on Why You Feel Bad About Yourself

There was nothing quite as terrifying as answering a question in class as a boy who suffered from self-esteem issues. It often felt as though I had been asked to present a speech in front of the whole school without preparation.

I mean, there you are, sitting in class, enjoying the lesson because it is a class that you love greatly. Let's say it's Biology. You spend all of your free time reading biology books and learning a lot about the subject and thus, you are pretty knowledgeable on the subject. However, when in class, each time the teacher asks a question, you somehow cannot bring yourself to raise your hand and answer it.

What if I am wrong? You ask yourself. *What if my classmates laugh at me for getting it wrong? What if I mess up when answering?* You begin overthinking, and as a result, you don't raise your hand because you don't want to make a mess and experience the shame of being judged by your classmates.

Or perhaps you are out in the field with your friends, and they decide to play basketball. You like basketball and enjoy playing it in your free time at home. Yet, now, with others around you, you begin to wonder whether you really are up to the task.

Am I that good at basketball? What if I fail the team, and my friends all laugh at me? What would I do if I missed the shot that would have granted my team the win? Will my friends still want to be with me?

Or maybe there is this girl in your math class that you have been crushing on for a while now. She seems friendly and nice enough, yet each time you decide that you want to talk to her, that voice of doubt creeps up again. *Am I good enough for her? What if she doesn't like the way I look, talk, or dress? What if she tells her friends I asked her out, and they all mock me behind my back?*

Or perhaps we could even look at a completely different scenario.

Your friends have decided that they want to skip class to do something else, perhaps go to the mall. While you have always fantasized about skipping classes, you have never truly pushed on with it. You may have had your rebellious moments but never compromised on classes. You would rather get in trouble for other reasons but not skip class.

Yet, when your friends inform you of the plan to skip class and ask you to join them, you find it hard to say no to them. *What if they stop speaking to me when I say no? What if they think I am a coward? What if they have more fun without me?*

So, you pretend to be someone you are not and join them, even though you absolutely do not want that.

You may have found yourself in situations like the above or similar situations where you desire to do one thing but then, are unable to do it because you do not have the confidence to follow through.

You want to answer that question in class but are fearful because you feel as though others would perhaps answer it better. You want to ask your crush out but are afraid that you may not be good enough for them or they may not like you for who you are. You want to say no to skipping class, but you also do not want to feel as though you don't belong, so you follow through with skipping class.

Your inability to do what you want to do in each of the above scenarios points to one thing – ***a lack of belief and confidence in who you are and what you stand for.***

It can feel overwhelming to be unable to be yourself or to find the confidence to do what you want to do, yet that is the path for us all. *But why exactly? Why am I feeling this way?* You wonder.

Why Teenage Boys Struggle with Self-Esteem

There could be various reasons as to why teenage boys struggle with self-esteem. Still, there are several universal reasons that often play a critical role in shaping teenage boys' perceptions of themselves. I am certain that you will recognize these and know how they impact your life.

- **Hormonal Changes**

Okay, this first point is something that is beyond your control.

As you grow, you are often undergoing a radical change in your body in ways that you have never experienced. Teenage years are considered transitional years because they are the years that mark the change from being a child to becoming an adult. Thus, *your body undergoes drastic changes*, often several concurrent changes all at once.

Suddenly, you begin to grow hair in unusual places; you begin to notice your voice changing; perhaps you begin to grow facial hair and are suddenly aware of your sexuality. You also begin to sweat a lot, and it doesn't smell nice. Then, you are also beginning to experience shifts in your moods, which you have no control over, and it all is too much to keep track of.

All these changes begin to affect you, and without proper guidance, they can overwhelm you and, thus, lead to you feeling ashamed of who you are and, consequently, developing self-esteem issues.

As mentioned, this cause for self-esteem is beyond your control, but as we will learn later in this book, you can control how you react to these hormonal changes.

- **Pressure to Conform**

I am sure you have all heard of the phrase *'boys will be boys.'*

I cannot tell you how much harm this simple phrase, often uttered whenever a boy does something considered 'masculine,' has done to the self-esteem of boys who do not fit into the mold of what makes a boy a 'boy.'

For example, I would often get into trouble simply because I followed my friends as they got into trouble because I felt as though that was what I needed to do to belong. I could not bring myself to say no to these friends of mine because then, would I really be a boy if I was not part of the group?

Or other times, I would stop myself from showing too many sensitive emotions for fear of appearing weak, especially in front of other boys. After all, I am sure you are aware of this notion that boys shouldn't show too much emotion as anyone who showed too much sentiments was looked at as less of a boy.

'Look, he's crying like a little girl.' I am sure that you have heard this sentiment at one point or another.

This is why, even with my friends, we never talked about our deepest desires and wants to each other and instead, our talks often centered around our interests and hobbies that we enjoyed doing and stopped at that. And often, these hobbies needed to be 'masculine.'

Now, I did enjoy a lot of things that could be considered masculine in my teenage years, but I also enjoyed simply doing simple things, like reading and writing, making simple art, and watching anime.

However, I was never confident enough to let my friends know this because I did not want them to think any less of me.

Perhaps this is you, too. Maybe you are *a calmer, less abrasive, more measured, and introverted person*, and this pressure to conform makes you begin to doubt your identity as a boy. You begin to feel as though you are a letdown as your current self and, thus, need to conform or be outed as not being enough of a boy.

For example, you may enjoy being by yourself, but then, because there is an expectation that boys need to be extroverts who are always going out and getting into trouble, you feel like you must do that.

Or maybe you do not enjoy watching action movies and instead prefer, let's say, watching fantasy movies. Because of the societal expectation that action movies are more masculine and, thus, are a rite of passage into manhood, you then also try to live up to this expectation of what you are supposed to be by watching these action movies, even if you don't enjoy them.

So, there you are, folding under the pressure of doing things that are considered to be more masculine so that you can 'prove' your masculinity to others.

These societal expectations thrust upon your shoulders in your teens will often create a disconnect between who you think you are supposed to be or who you think society wants you to be and who you really are. This disconnect, then, often leads to self-doubts and low self-esteem.

- **Attack on Identity**

As the transitional years into adulthood, your teenage years are the years in which your identity matters a lot to you.

You want to belong somewhere, and this desire is so strong that nothing else matters. Say you love video games and so, you try to align yourself with others who also like video games.

We often form very strong bonds in our teenage years based on how well we identify with our peers or how well we want to identify with our peers. This is why peer pressure is a common issue among teenagers. The *desire to find an identity often causes some teenagers to simply do anything,* including betraying their true selves, just to find an identity that they lack elsewhere.

Thus, when you are constantly attacked for who you are, when what makes you relate to others your age is constantly mocked, it can lead to a drop in self-esteem.

This attack on your identity to meet societal expectations might cause you to try and change your identity into one that is more acceptable to society at large. Like for example, you might begin to try and act more aggressively just so you can fit into the ideal frame of what you have been told masculinity is.

When you feel as though your identity will result in you getting attacked, you often will then try to hide it and live your life as is expected of boys your age, which also causes a rift between who you are and who you are supposed to be. This rift is what chips away at your confidence.

- **Unattainable Ideal Man Credentials**

The movies, TV shows, advertisements, and even social media are often awash with an idealized portrayal of who an ideal man is supposed to be. This ideal man is supposed to have *a sharp jawline, piercing blue eyes, a set of immaculate white teeth, and a chiseled body*. They also must be *outgoing and aggressive* and should *not show any strong emotions, except maybe for anger.*

You see this 'man' everywhere. They are the action hero and protagonists of many movies and TV shows in advertisements for anything targeted towards men and even women. On social media, the men who most closely resemble this aesthetic are the ones who get the largest following and seem to have the most people swooning over them in the comment section.

This portrayal of this version of the ideal man creates an unrealistic image of what a man is and what he is supposed to look like and behave; at the age that you are, this message will often leave an impact, and the impact is a negative one.

When you don't meet the criteria of who you should be as a man based on this portrayal, it leaves you feeling worthless. If you are an introverted boy who doesn't have an athletic body type and is also quite sensitive, you will feel as though there is something wrong with you because why aren't you like this ideal man?

The above are some of the most common reasons why many boys your age suffer from a feeling of worthlessness. I want you to know that while I understand that it is inevitable that all the above will be present in your life no matter how hard you try to hide from it, you also need to be aware of the fact that you can learn to become yourself amidst all these issues.

Your desire to fit in, your feelings of not being true to yourself because of external pressure, and the strong pull to prove yourself are all very valid, and in order to overcome these feelings, you need to learn how to be okay with who you are first.

Chapter 2: Self-Validation - Why You Should Embrace the Struggle

Shame. That is the one feeling that often marks our feelings of low self-worth.

This is **the feeling that makes you want to crawl into a hole whenever you are put on the spot**. This is what you feel whenever you are made aware of your flaws, either intentionally or not. That moment when you suddenly become aware that you lack confidence, when you see your crush and can't approach her, or when you seem not to be able to express how you feel, it is that *shame takes root*, and this is very damaging.

Because we are held hostage by our beliefs that we are not worthy of other people's time, because we live for the approval of our peers, and due to the strong desire to fit in no matter what, we often experience a crippling feeling of shame over who we are and our struggles.

But I want you to hold it right there.

Allowing shame to overtake you will only make you feel worse about yourself. The constant desire to escape who you are means that you will never truly understand who you are in order to know what to change. In this chapter, I will give you reasons why you should embrace the struggle and validate the emotions you are feeling as a radical way to alter your way of thinking later.

Self-Esteem Struggles Are Universal

When you are struggling with being confident in who you are and standing up for what you believe in, I want you to understand that you should not feel ashamed of that because, you know what? *Many people also struggle with asserting themselves.*

Okay, I know what you are thinking - How is that supposed to make me feel better?

Here is why.

When you begin to think that the issues you face are unique to you and that every other person has it figured out and you haven't, you then view it as a sign of weakness or failure on your part. You begin to view everything that you fail at doing as a personal failure.

You think that your inability to say no is you being the biggest coward in the world. Your inability to approach your crush means you are a creep who will end up alone forever, and so on.

This further then *makes you even more self-conscious of your issues*, which further compounds them and makes them even worse.

However, understanding that what you are going through is universal **helps put things into perspective and makes it easier for you to want to change** that. This is what worked for me and I think it also would work for you.

Just think of how much better you feel when you learn that some of your favorite pop stars went through the same struggles that you did. It often gives you a small boost of confidence, doesn't it?

Despite being a star at an early age, Justin Bieber struggled so much with his self-esteem that, to this day, he suffers from depression. In fact, his self-esteem became worse after he became famous because then, he had to live up to the societal expectations of growing up to be a male 'sex symbol' in the full glare of the general public. The pressure to fit into the ideal male standards rested heavily on him after he became famous. However, he managed to overcome these and is now living his life as best as he can.

Or for example, Mr. Beast (Jimmy Donaldson), the world's biggest YouTuber. Mr. Beast had known since an early age that he wanted to do YouTube. This was because, at 14/15, he saw other people on YouTube quit their jobs and create video content full-time. He wanted to be on camera even though, as a child, he was introverted.

However, his parents, like most parents, wanted him to go to college and get a normal job. The pressure between wanting to be who he was and what his parents wanted weighed heavily on him, so much that his mother even threatened to kick him out, which must have been hard on the young Jimmy.

Despite all this, Jimmy was able to fulfill his dreams of becoming a YouTuber and now even uses his platform to give back to society through his various philanthropic ventures.

Or take Khaby Lame, for example, who is the most followed person on TikTok and one of the most influential young people around. The 24-year-old was laid off from his factory work during the 2020 COVID period. Low on confidence and with nothing else to do, Lame decided to try his hands on

TikTok. He wanted to create content that would reach as many people as possible.

Except, there was a problem - he could only speak Italian, and the only people who watched his earlier videos were his father and neighbor. But rather than let this stop him, he instead decided to simply make content without speaking, letting his facial expressions and body language speak for him. And that is how he went viral, through using his body to make his point, often breaking down over-complicated life hack videos into simple actions.

The above examples show you that what you are going through is something that even the people we admire went through and perhaps are still going through.

That is the perspective that I want you to consider each time you feel bad about yourself – that there are others, including people we admire, who struggled with who they were and what society wants them to be, then ***chose to follow their paths and did great.***

Thus, find comfort in knowing that other teens are struggling with the same things that you are, and you will find that this shifts your perspective. Even the most confident athletic boy in class or the most beautiful girl in class, no matter how confident they appear, all have issues they are struggling with. Sure, maybe to a lesser degree than you, but still, it's there.

Understanding this gives you a perspective that:

1. You are not a failure for feeling the way you do.

2. There is always a way out.

It is Your Brain, Not You

The reason you are feeling the way you are is not because there is something wrong with you but rather because *your brain is changing.*

The significant development in the brain occurs at the region of the brain called the ***prefrontal cortex***, which is the part of the brain that is often tasked with *decision-making and self-regulation.*

This part of your brain will often be maturing during your teen years. During this significant maturity process, it usually then means that, naturally you become much more self-conscious and struggle with managing how you feel as the self-regulatory part begins to take shape.

So, there is nothing wrong with you even as you experience a lack of strong belief in yourself – it simply is part of growing up, so don't beat yourself too much. Accept how you feel, and you will have an easier time getting over those feelings.

It Is a Chance for Growth

Throughout this period of facing self-esteem issues, it can often feel overwhelming. However, I want you to know that these feelings that you are experiencing are an opportunity for you to grow and build resilience within you.

I don't want to sit here and offer you empty platitudes on how 'adversity builds resilience' and whatnot, but rather, I want you to know that ***when you feel bad about yourself, you now have a chance and a choice to change that for the better.***

Because your experiences with how you feel and perceive yourself are down to your maturing brain and, thus, will mostly be beyond your control, it is still a chance for you to learn more about other ways in which you can become a better person.

For example, you may not be able to stop yourself from your emotional impulses because that is simply the brain firing due to hormonal changes, but you can learn how to regulate them.

Or perhaps you may not completely get rid of the feeling that you are letting other people down or that somehow you are not worth their time. Still, your emotional regulation could make you build better relationships, which put more emphasis on your strengths than weaknesses, thus, helping you feel better about yourself.

Additionally, you may also become a lot more empathetic and understanding to your peers who are experiencing similar things that you are going through. When you struggle and are aware of the struggle and pull yourself out of it, you then become better equipped to support your friends who might be going through something similar.

Through empathy, you also strengthen relationships, which further help you become more confident, creating this cycle of positivity that feeds in itself, further helping make you more confident.

You Don't Need to Be Perfect to be Confident

Another reason why you should not be too hard on yourself because of your flaws and weaknesses is that you don't need to be perfect or flawless to be confident.

This is a very big misconception that I believed during my teens and which I know many, like you, believe too. This belief is that you need to be utterly flawless in order to be perfect. Certainly, that is often what TV shows and movies always seem to portray.

Whenever there is a character lacking in confidence, it is often because they usually have a flaw that they are extremely conscious about, thus making them feel like they are of no value. But then, when they become more confident, it usually is because they have gotten rid of this flaw or flaws that they had.

I know you can name movies with such messages, even if it's not in the text, but in subtext. Such media portrayal of what confidence means – lacking flaws or perfection – perpetuates the myth that to be confident, you must rid yourself of all your flaws and imperfections.

However, I am here to tell you that that is not true. You don't need to be perfect to be confident. You don't need to feel your best to be confident, nor do you need to be completely confident about everything about yourself. Confidence *is about being aware of your flaws and imperfections, changing what you can about them, but choosing to be confident anyway because of your strengths.*

This is why, then, you should not be too hard on yourself because of your imperfections and flaws. The reason you feel that way is because of the conditioning that you have been exposed to, and when you begin to embrace who you are, flaws, and all, you give room for true confidence to take root.

Confidence is a Process, Not an End Goal

Another reason that you shouldn't be too hard on yourself for lacking confidence is because being confident is not an end goal that you reach, and that's it. Rather, it is a process that you will **need to constantly update from time to time** to match your new philosophies in life, new life milestones or simply to adapt to the changes in how your brain perceives confidence and the world around you.

Here is a secret that perhaps you may not know – even the most confident people that you know always have moments of self-doubt, of feeling as though they are not good enough or worthy enough of what they are getting.

Sometimes, you just have bad days, and that is okay, but these bad days should not stop you from understanding that you are on the right path to building confidence in yourself.

Noah Schnapp is one of the most prominent young people in the world right now who gained fame from playing Will Byers in the hit show *Stranger Things*. He is also very big on TikTok. Noah, 21, had this to say about having bad days:

"We all have bad days, but it's important to find the silver lining and keep moving forward."

Noah reminds us that while we won't always feel at our best each day, we need always to find the reason to keep moving forward and doing things that help us become better people.

But it's not just stars who have days when they are not completely confident. Adults around you do it, too. Yet, more often than not, you will never be able to tell this. Do you know why?

It is because they understand that being confident is something that, yes, you learn how to build, but also, you need to find ways to reinforce constantly from time to time. Because the circumstances around you are continually changing, things are constantly evolving, you also need to evolve your confidence with the changes so that your self-doubt does not have enough room to take root.

Thus, you need to be aware of the reality that those feelings of low self-worth, the feeling that you are letting other people down or that you do not have what it takes to do one thing or another, will always be there to some degree. When you are ashamed about these feelings, then you may never truly be confident.

Instead, **embrace confidence as** the choice to shift your focus on what your strengths are and what you are good at, as the choice to adapt to your environment and try your best to remain true to yourself to the best of your ability and knowledge. True confidence is hearing that voice tell you, 'You can't do it/you are not worthy' and choosing to do it still or believe in yourself because your belief in what you are good at will be stronger than these voices of doubt.

The emotional states that you are experiencing are all feelings that normal human beings experience, and thus, you are not alone. When you embrace how you feel, when you acknowledge that your feelings of low self-worth are valid, you then give yourself an opportunity to see a way out. And the first step towards finding a way out is through self-discovery.

Chapter 3: Self-Discovery – Digging Deep into Your Shell to Find Yourself

During my time as a teen, I always found myself asking this question: *Who am I really? Like, what makes me who I am?*

Through asking myself this question, I began to wonder if I at all had anything that was uniquely me, that made me stand out as an individual, and it became clear that I needed to find an answer to this question before forging an identity that didn't reflect whom I truly was and having a hard time changing it later on.

This is perhaps where you, too, are now.

You are now beginning to form your identity outside that which your parents gave you as a much younger child. You're beginning to learn about what it means to be independent, to want to do things on your own.

Yet, I am also aware of the reality that because of the pressure that you face, you will very quickly lose sight of who you are during this part of your life. That desire for independence could easily turn into isolation, and wanting to do things on your own could easily become an obsession that costs you valuable relationships.

Because of the precarious state that being a teenage boy is, you need then to have a solid foundation and understanding of yourself so that you can discern what helps you become more independent vs. what is isolating you from others, what it means to want to be accepted for who you are vs. trying to be who you are not just to fit in.

But first, why is self-discovery very important to building self-esteem?

Why Self-Discovery is Key to Becoming More Confident

Self-discovery is a hack to becoming much more comfortable with who you are because of very many reasons, and below are some of them:

- **You Understand Your Strengths and Weaknesses Better**

The unfortunate reality is that as a teen boy, you are often wandering through your teenage years without ever finding out what you are good at; you only get to know what you are bad at and are self-conscious about. This is perhaps because the people around you, especially adults, may only be focusing on pointing out your flaws and failings and doing little to bring awareness to what you are good at.

These extreme levels of self-consciousness are what made my teen years a living nightmare because there I was, extremely self-conscious and thus, only saw myself in a negative light. Seeing myself through the lenses of my flaws, flaws that others around me always pointed out and, thus, etched them permanently in my psyche.

Perhaps you read that previous paragraph and thought, *'Wait, I also feel the same.'* You tend to lean into your self-consciousness so much that you become an expert at what you are bad at. If someone asks you to name your main flaws, you can list them even in your sleep.

You are too deep into what you are failing at and what you lack, whether it be physically, academically, emotionally, mentally, or otherwise. The more you shine this harsh spotlight onto your weaknesses, the less confident you feel about yourself, and this creates a vicious cycle that leaves you almost pulling your head out, wondering, *'When will it all end?'*

Well, it ends, or in other words, the journey to recovery begins with self-discovery. Digging within yourself helps you take time off from simply combing through your flaws with a tooth comb to actually ***understanding yourself holistically, uncovering things deep within yourself*** you never knew you were capable of.

Sure, some of these things you uncover might be negative, reinforcing what you have already been told, but you will also discover unique talents, strengths, and interests, which can help give you a boost in how you feel about yourself. Just imagine spending time in self-discovery and finding out that you have a talent for music, or perhaps you have a knack for problem-solving, or maybe that you are a good listener.

That will make you feel better about yourself, won't it?

- **You Embrace Your Individuality**

I know that during this time of your life, nothing matters more than getting accepted by your peers and gaining their respect and admiration. I get that because that was what shaped my entire teenage years – seeking the approval of others.

But there is a saying that I like that says:

When we approve of ourselves, rather than always seeking approval, we find happiness.

Let me put you at ease by saying that this point isn't to make you reject wanting to be with your peers.

Rather, when you enter into a journey of self-discovery, you will understand yourself better: know what you like or dislike, what you want or don't want in a friend, and what your values are. Through knowing these things then, **you will find it easier to associate with people who align with these things that matter to you.**

So, you will no longer simply be trying to please your friends who want to skip school, but rather, you will find friends who help you do better in class because that is what you also want. You will also become more confident in speaking to others because you will be speaking from a place of knowing who you are, and I think that's cool.

- **You Recognize Limiting Beliefs**

'I am not good enough,' 'I'll never be as good at math as Jamie,' 'My crush will never like me for who I am.'

These are all limiting beliefs we tend to have when we lack self-esteem, and they often come from a lack of support. The lack of support and help then shape our beliefs, and these limiting beliefs almost always settle until adulthood, which poses a greater challenge to change.

Many men out here might seem like they have it all together, but I can tell you with confidence that many of them are working hard to rid themselves of the limiting beliefs that settled into their psyche during their teen years.

Thus, when you embrace self-discovery, you embrace introspection, and introspection shines a spotlight on these limiting beliefs and makes you aware of some of the lines of thoughts that are chipping away at your confidence *so that it is easy for you to root out these beliefs* when you decide to do so.

The thing about self-discovery is that, while it seems like this complicated thing that could keep you away from others for a long time as you try to find yourself, it is actually something that you can do without ever skipping a heartbeat.

You can incorporate self-discovery techniques into your daily routine, make it part of hanging out with your friends, part of your downtime at home, and so on.

Below are some activities that will help you learn more about yourself without breaking from your daily life:

Simple Ways to Finding Yourself

Finding yourself is all about finding the strength and courage to be authentic and make choices to show up and be true to yourself.

One of the quotes that I like goes like this, *'Authenticity is a collection of choices that we have to make every day. It's about the choice to show up and be real.'*

Below are some of the choices that you can make:

- **Practice Activities That Bring Attention to Your Inner Emotional State**

Finding yourself is often not a process that you begin by taking the biggest action, but rather, it is built on starting small, and the best way to start small is to begin doing activities that direct attention inward.

The process of finding who you truly are is like building muscle – it takes practice.

Now, remember I said that these are things that you can do easily without breaking your routine. Here are some simple ways to discover your inner self:

1. Introspection

Do you ever want to just sit down and think through things that matter to you, like actually thinking through them and not just brush over them with a second or two of thought?

That is what introspection is all about – *sitting and thinking deeply about yourself as a person,* about your emotional and mental processes, the actions they determine, and more.

The early memories of myself when I began thinking more deeply about myself were brutal. I remember being completely stunned by just how negative that voice inside my head was, and I also began making a connection between this negative voice and my actions.

The voice went a little something like this:

'The reason you are failing is because you are just a loser, nothing more. There is nothing to think about.'

'The reason you cannot raise your hand in class is because you are a clown.'

'You are having a hard time making friends because no one wants to be friends with someone as boring as you.'

I mean, I don't know about you, but that's a little too harsh. Nobody would ever have confidence if that were the voice whispering to their ears each day.

These voices were constant, and they were loud and they were a significant reason why I was always down on confidence. So, when I sat down to introspect, I always looked at myself through these critical lenses.

I tried to counter these thoughts by constantly trying to prove them wrong, but it all failed. Reason? I always started my journey inwards through these critical lenses.

See, while introspection is important to self-discovery, you need to **introspect with curiosity, not criticism.**

I always let this negative voice be the one to guide me as I thought, and that is why I never truly managed to make any progress until I learned to, instead, begin my journey inwards through the lenses of curiosity rather than criticism and blame.

Oh, I think that I am a loser. Okay. Why is that? Why do I think I am a loser?

Why do I think that I am a clown, and how does this affect my ability to contribute in class?

Why do I think I am boring and how does this self-fulfil in how I interact with those around me?

By changing my introspection questions to the 'why' behind the negative thought, I was able to find out a lot about myself, both positive and negative.

So, at the end of each day, find a place to sit quietly, clear yourself of any distractions, and begin to think through your thoughts.

Ask yourself, *why do I believe that I am not worthy of love? How did this thought come to be?* Then, begin to encourage yourself to let go of this thought by giving yourself words of affirmation.

For example, if you find out that you think you are not worthy of love just because you think you are not good-looking enough, try to find positive things you like about yourself and focus your mind on these things.

2. *Drawing*

Well, this might seem ridiculous, but drawing does actually help you figure out things about yourself that you don't know, especially if you are artistically inclined or if you simply enjoy the process of just doodling when thinking through stuff.

So, don't shy away from picking a pencil or pen and drawing stuff when you are thinking deeply. Through drawing, you can bring to the fore deep lying issues within yourself that you otherwise could not express. Pick up that piece of paper and begin to draw those doodles as you think. You will be stunned at what they reveal.

3. *Journaling*

Journaling is one of the best ways that you can check in on yourself because you are reliving the events of a day while looking back at them like an outside observer. Journaling, especially before bed, helps give you perspective on who you are, how you act, and how you handle your emotions, and this can help you become better.

For example, write down about your day. Write *how different activities, interactions, and events throughout the day made you feel.* When you journal for a long enough time, you will begin to get a picture of who you are based on how these different happenings make you feel.

The above are some examples of activities that you can incorporate into your routine to help you understand yourself better. You can add other activities not mentioned here as long as they are activities that grant you some time to be alone, even for a little while.

- **Figure Out Your Values and Beliefs**

Another simple way to find yourself is to know your values.

Through digging deep into what shapes your thoughts and actions, you may find the values and beliefs you hold dearest.

Let us begin by looking at what values are.

Our ***values are a very strong indicator of who we are deep inside*** when no one else is looking. They are often positive, such as compassion, honesty, loyalty, creativity, and the like. Our values determine the actions that we take, whether knowingly or unknowingly.

However, since you want to know who you are, then you need to understand how your values *reflect your actions knowingly* and this can then help you understand yourself better so that you know where to improve.

Beliefs, on the other hand, encompasses both positive and negative ways of thinking. As someone struggling with their perception of who they are, you will find a lot of negative beliefs about yourself. These beliefs will often be a twisting of our values due to negative reinforcement.

For example, let's say you find out that honesty is one of your strongest values. Due to negative reinforcement, however, your belief is that you are honest because you are a coward who cannot lie. Perhaps you came to hold this belief because you are constantly bombarded with messages that reinforce the idea that honesty isn't that important to a man or a boy.

Or if you are compassionate, you may believe that this is a sign of weakness in you because the message from all around you, from the media, from other boys and men, is that men showing the vulnerability of compassion are exposing themselves to ridicule and being taken advantage of.

To figure out your values, begin to take note of your actions and ask yourself:

1. What values that I hold dear did that action represent? If the action didn't represent any values you hold dear, why then did you do it?

2. What beliefs does this action represent? For example, when you constantly put yourself down, it represents the belief that you think you are less worthy of other people's attention and affection.

3. Where did this belief emerge from? Often, it comes from our environment, but where exactly should be your main concern? This way, you will begin to become more observant of your environment and will then be able to pick out the ways in which it is not aligning with the values you wish to embody and, thus, change them, as we will learn through the rest of the book.

When you become aware of these deep-seated beliefs and values, you give yourself a platform to then work on improving yourself from there. Keep in mind, though, that this probably won't stop you from constantly seeking the approval of your peers, as that is a part of growing up. Still, the more you understand yourself, the better you will become at knowing how to identify things that make you feel worse about yourself and those that make you feel better and make the best choice.

Once you dig deep into your shell to find yourself, the next step is using what you have discovered about who you are to make yourself a better person.

Chapter 4: Finding Your Hobbies and Passion and How They Make You Feel Better

I once met a young boy whom I will call Alex. Alex was never confident about anything in himself.

Because of this lack of confidence then, he had resigned to being in the shadows, often seeming contented to just be the person going with the flow, never truly asserting who they were anywhere: not in class, not with his friends, not even with his family.

However, what I noticed about Alex was that he was very good at drawing for a person of his age. His drawings were often almost close to what you see in comic books, and I was stunned when he mentioned to me that he never truly felt as though they were good enough to show other people.

I respected that and never tried to convince him to share his art when he wasn't ready, but then I asked him how he felt whenever he was drawing.

"I feel like myself," he said, *"I feel as though I have control of my life and that I am capable of doing great things."*

That statement, right there, was what I needed to hear – the fact that something so innocuous could give him such high levels of confidence, even if for a brief moment, gave me something to work with as I helped him build his confidence.

This could also be you. Whether it is drawing art, playing sports, photography, or whatever you enjoy doing for the peace of mind can be a great connecting thread between your current self and your future confident self.

Nothing ever builds your sense of pride in yourself than doing something that you want to do and doing it to the best of your ability.

But how does this work? You may be wondering. Why do hobbies and passion matter in building confidence?

Why Hobbies and Passion Are Key in Building Esteem

Hobbies provide us with an escape from the world we are experiencing, giving us a chance to simply engage in something, not out of desperation, not out of compulsion, but simply out of *personal fulfillment*. Doing something out of personal fulfillment often gives us the biggest boost in self-belief that we can ever hope for.

Developing your hobbies and passion can be an enriching experience because of several factors, which include:

• They Are Fun

I mean, who wouldn't want to have fun? Even when you are struggling with self-doubt and feelings of inadequacy, there is no doubt that doing something that you often enjoy gives you a reason to smile. Think of the last time you did something that made you very happy.

Did you have fun? How long did it take you to forget everything and just live in the moment? Did you even think about your struggles? Perhaps even if you did think about what you were struggling with, you still allowed yourself to get lost in the fun of what you were doing at that moment.

Sure, having fun doing things you enjoy doesn't directly translate into having high esteem for a lifetime. But it certainly is a good place to start.

• Give You a Sense of Accomplishment

Whether it is something as simple as learning how to cook or completing a project that you have always wanted to complete, hobbies provide you with opportunities to do things that you enjoy doing. As you continually work on these things, you experience a sense of joy and pride each time you make progress.

This sense of accomplishment often makes you feel good about yourself, and this confidence, born from the sense of pride in completing a project, will often spill over to other areas of your life, thus making you feel better about yourself in general.

- **Hobbies Provide You With Opportunities for Personal Growth**

We often lose self-esteem because we tend to feel a sense of stagnation in our lives at this time. Rapid milestones and growth often mark the years preceding teenage years. You quickly go from crawling to walking before you know it. You go from making nonsensical noises to speaking within months.

Then, before you know it, you are in elementary school. Within a few years, you are in middle school, all this as you rapidly outgrow your previous clothes, interests, and other things.

When you are a teen looking back at these major milestones you hit previously, you can feel as though now that you are a teen, things have slowed down a bit. Sure, your body is experiencing significant changes, but there is often that feeling that you are not living quite up to expectations, and this feeling chips away at your confidence little by little.

This is where hobbies, passion, and talent come in. They become areas where you can explore different parts of yourself and learn how to grow and become a better person through different accomplishments and progress you make in your hobbies.

- **Provide You With an Avenue to Relieve Stress**

Class is stressing you out; school projects are piling up; you are also stressing about whether your friends will find out that you are merely pretending to like certain things. You are also stressed about how best to approach your crush so they don't reject you.

All this can become a little too much, and you just want to let go of the stress and unwind for a little bit.

This is where hobbies come in.

Hobbies that allow self-expression, like art and writing, or those that give you a boost of confidence, like dancing, are very effective in helping you unwind and let go of any stress that you may be experiencing.

These hobbies allow you, even if it is for a few minutes a day, to let go of the mental anguish and lose yourself in what you are doing for the joy of it. That sense of relaxation allows your body to calm down and for the anxiety to drop, which then means that the next time you are out there, you will be much calmer and be able to think more clearly and make better decisions.

- **Give You Avenues to Connect With Like-Minded People**

Hobbies can also give you a platform to connect with other like-minded people and this can be a big boost to how you feel about yourself.

Hear me out; I know that as a self-conscious teen, some hobbies like the ones where you have to be with many other people might perhaps seem like they could be an avenue for making you feel worse about yourself, but I can assure you that that is not the case.

In my life until now, what I have learned is that *many people are often welcoming to new people who have similar interests* to them most of the time, and so, when you get a chance to connect with like-minded people who enjoy similar hobbies as yours, and they are welcoming to you, take that chance.

Hobbies such as hiking, joining a book club if you enjoy reading, volunteering, running, cycling, and others provide you with an opportunity to be part of a community where you can nerd out about this thing that you love doing without fear of judgment. Doing this provides you with a positive self-image because you are in the company of people who enjoy this activity as much as you do.

These communities also allow you to practice your social skills and the more comfortable you become talking to others, the more your overall self-confidence is enhanced.

But how can I explore these hobbies and passions? How do I find out what I enjoy and what I don't?

How to Find Your Passion and Pick a Hobby

- **Try Different Activities**

Look, I understand that you feel bad about yourself and are not sure about who you are and what you stand for, but if you want to rid yourself of that feeling, you will need to power through the doubts and get going.

Engaging in different activities is a great and fun way to find out which activities you enjoy doing and which you don't. After all, you are a teenage boy, so why should you hold yourself back out of fear when you can find yourself through experimentation?

Go out there and join the art club, then try the writing club, drama, and theatre, maybe. Whatever it is that you do, t*he goal is to find an activity that resonates with you despite your fears.*

Therefore, when seeking out a hobby, ***keep an open mind and be curious*** to try out new activities. Who knows, perhaps something that you previously had thought was a waste of your time, could become a passion of yours if given a chance.

Through engaging in different activities, you give yourself a chance to find those that deeply resonate with you, and when you do, you will find great joy in your life.

- **Pick Something Fun for You**

It is very easy to pick a hobby simply because you want to follow a particular trend. And I believe that perhaps, due to the low confidence you are experiencing, you might pick your hobby based on trends so that you can feel like you belong.

However, I want you to know that there is no perfect hobby or passion project. Sure, some passion projects might have a higher chance of becoming a useful skill, but it is important that you pick a hobby that will be fun to you, one that is *deeply related to your interests and values.*

If, for example, you enjoy reading a lot, then writing as a hobby could be perfect, or joining a book club to discuss your favorite book. If, for instance, you feel like you are very compassionate and want to help others, then volunteering can be the way to go.

Whatever it is you choose as your hobby, ensure that it always aligns with what you already enjoy. This will make the hobby more fun, rather than simply picking what's popular.

Sure, you can still try out popular hobbies as part of the experimentation process, but *don't settle for it simply due to its popularity*. Pick it because it is fun and in line with what you have always wanted to do.

So, with each activity that you try out, give it a few sessions and then take notes. Ask yourself, *'Through it all, have I been enjoying this? What do I love about it, and what don't I love about it? Can I enjoy this activity despite its shortcomings?'*

If, after several tries, you still can't find any enjoyment in it, then let it go and try something else until you find one or two or three that are fun and make you happy.

- **Brainstorm with Those Around You**

One of the ways that I discovered that I had an inclination towards being compassionate was through speaking with family and friends. They spoke about how I always tried to help. They also mentioned that I had a knack for problem-solving and writing, and that is how I managed to find my hobbies.

Sit down with your friends and ask them what things you often show great interest in. If you do not have friends, then ask family members. I know that speaking to your parents is hard, especially as a teenage boy with self-esteem issues, but they can give you insight into what things have interested you since early in your life. You can also speak with your siblings and ask them what they have observed about things you like to do.

If you do not have many friends or siblings, then do not fret.

- **Check Your Journals**

If you are keeping a journal of your daily events, then you can re-read them and try to pick out the things that appear the most in your journal, depending on how you feel about them. Usually, we tend not to see the pattern of how we behave until we look back, connect the dots, and see the big picture.

While you may not capture every single thing that you do daily in your journal, there is no doubt that things that matter the most to us, things that are memorable to us, sometimes good or bad, will often make it into these journals.

Thus, look for those things, activities, and interests which you write about constantly and which make you feel good. They can give you a good hint of where your next hobby or your passion project could be.

Take your time, read your journals, and ask yourself:

1. What are the things that I talk about the most in my journal?

2. What are the emotions I have expressed on these things? Happiness? Contentment? A sense of wonder and adventure?

3. If they make me happy, contented, and satisfied, how can I turn them into a hobby?

Sometimes, even journaling can become a hobby in and of itself and could transition into writing which can help you learn more about self-expression, and self-expression is a great sign of confidence.

The thing about having a hobby is that you will never pretend about it. Activities that you enjoy will find their way into your life simply because you will naturally be drawn to them.

Thus, as you try out various activities that you can turn into hobbies, remember that this is not something that you should do because you need to or because you think it is the only way to build your self-esteem. First and foremost, *seek a hobby because it is something that you like and because it will be fun.*

Let the whims of the activity that you choose carry you into a world beyond the one you are currently occupying. By the time you return to this world, you will have made one more step towards becoming much more self-assured.

As you work through your hobbies, next, we cover how you can build confidence through caring for your physical and mental health.

Chapter 5: Caring for Your Physical and Mental Health

I never played sports, nor was I even mildly athletic in my teenage years, and thus, I was very conscious of this fact and often tried to hide my body under layers and layers of cloth. If people never truly saw my body, then they would not make fun of me, I thought.

This level of self-consciousness, then, meant that, more often than not, I would simply avoid taking part in any athletic or physical activity, even if I wanted to, because I thought that I did not have the body to display for others to see. I thought I looked like a blob, and who wants to see that?

What I was not aware of, though, was that the belief that I needed to have this perfect body in order to wear the clothes that I wanted to wear to play the sports I wanted to was also making me extremely miserable, which then further made me even more insecure about my body, creating this vicious cycle of negative mental state feeding into the physical state which then further fed into my mental state and so on.

Does the above story hit home or somewhere close to home?

Maybe you may not be as extreme as I was, but the fact that you are having self-esteem issues means that you are extremely conscious of your body to some degree. It often happens, as a teenage boy, to experience some disconnect from your body and view it through negative and unflattering lenses.

During this period in our lives, we are often undergoing various physical and emotional changes, and these changes shape how we view ourselves and our confidence. This is what is called body image, and our body images shape how we perceive our own physical appearance, including our overall attractiveness, body shape, and size.

Why We Struggle With Body Image Issues

Do you often look at yourself in the mirror? If not, why?

And if you do look at yourself in the mirror, do you like what you see? If not, why don't you like it? What is it about your body that makes you not like it?

I want you to answer these questions openly and honestly because they will help you understand how you relate to your body.

Now, I want you to think of your perceived flaws and then think back to how you came to view them as such.

The thing is, we are often very highly susceptible to *the influences from media and society at large* about our bodies and the beauty standards we are supposed to meet. I'll call back to the ideal male body standard and say that *the pressure to fit into that standard* often shapes our perception of our physical self and, thus, leads to us viewing our bodies through negative lenses.

When we become extremely preoccupied with our appearances, this then also affects other parts of our being, including our mental health. This is how we end up engaging in self-critical thoughts and behavior, which includes an unhealthy comparison with others and seeking validation from others just to feel something.

I mean, how many times have you looked at the older boys in school or the athletic students out in the field and thought that you look worse in comparison? How often have you envied the other boys in school who seem to fit perfectly into their clothes while you pull around heavy jackets and sweaters because you feel as though your body does not match theirs?

Here are some ways that can help you slowly begin to release yourself from this shackle of negative body image.

Building Confidence in Your Physical Self

Here is the thing that many people will never tell you about the human body – ***there is no perfect body***. There never has been, and there never will be. All of our bodies simply follow a natural order, and thus, there will always be something that one person will consider a flaw in their body.

Look at the other boys that you admire or envy because they seem to have the perfect body according to societal expectations. Chances are very high that they still have things about their body that they are not too fond of.

Below, then, is how to build confidence in your physical self without believing that you need to be perfect for that:

- **Accept Yourself**

Yes, I know it's a cliché. Yes, I know you may have heard it before, but consider this – the fact that it's a cliché means that it bears some truth.

Let's keep it real - how are you going to be comfortable in your own skin if you are always trying to escape it? How are you ever going to be confident in yourself if, first and foremost, you are not confident in your own body?

So, take a moment and stand in front of the mirror and look at yourself. Look at what you consider flaws and think, is there a chance that your 'flaws' and 'imperfections' are what make your body unique?

Because yes, there is a chance. Your body is unlike any other boy's body, and if nothing else gives you some joy, then revel in the knowledge that your body is unique to you only.

Now, I am not saying that you should not want to improve yourself physically. Rather, when you accept yourself for who you are, when you accept your body for what it is, then when eventually you decide to work out, it will come from *a genuine place of self-improvement*, not just so that you can meet some arbitrary beauty standards.

Even then, when you decide to work on improving your body,

- **Focus on Overall Body Health, Not Just Appearance**

Once again, let me begin by saying that your desire to have a great body is not invalid, but I want you to stop and ask yourself – What really does a great body mean to you? And this meaning of a great body, is it based on what you want or based on what society has told you through movies and TV shows?

If the body you want is based on societal ideals of male beauty standards, then I am sorry, but you are in for a big disappointment. Do you know why? *Beauty standards are always changing.*

We always hear about female beauty standards, but male beauty standards are also always changing, and the fact that they are rarely spoken about means that many young boys and men like you are never aware of this and, therefore, are constantly altering their bodies from time to time, not at all aware that you are altering your body for an ever-changing ideal.

Maybe today, abs might be considered attractive, but then, tomorrow, 'dad bods' are in vogue. Today beards might be attractive, but then tomorrow, it's that baby face with no facial hair. This fade might be trendy and hot today, but then tomorrow, that other fade is trendy, and there you are, following these trends without thought as you try to meet these arbitrary dynamics.

Lean in and let me whisper a little secret into your ear – rather than obsessing about appearance, try to improve your overall body health. When you focus on improving your overall body health, ***you will change your body based on what you desire rather than external pressure.***

I cannot tell you how learning to improve my overall health rather than just purely aesthetics helped me become more confident in my body. It all started with a simple alteration – I began caring about what I ate.

No, I did not go on some strict diet regimen (that is a whole other can of worms, believe me), but rather, I simply began to eat more of the homemade meals from my parents and minimized take-outs.

The simple action of eating the healthy variety of foods my parents made changed my whole relationship with myself. I suddenly began feeling much better about my body simply because the healthy foods that I ate improved my mood greatly.

This did not give me abs, nor did it make my beard grow faster, but it certainly made me look healthier. Thus, rather than frown at your parents or guardian feeding you veggies for a third day in a row, know that it will help improve your body health and that is worth something.

- **Become More Physically Active**

I just know that on reading the title, your mind immediately went to you sweating rivers in the gym as you lift weights. And if that is what you actually want to do, then by all means, do it.

However, what I meant about being more physically active is that you should begin to move around a lot more. It's that simple sometimes.

I am sure you are aware of *wearable technology*, which are the smart watches that people are using to keep tabs on their daily physical activity. Perhaps some of your peers who have smart watches might actually be doing this, looking to hit a certain number of steps in a day.

I am sorry to say this, but as annoying as these '10k-steps-a-day' people can be, they are actually right - being physically active, including just walking more, actually does wonders to your body and overall mood and consequently self-perception.

See, when you engage in any physical activity that burns calories, including walking and jogging, your body releases endorphins, which are feel-good hormones. These hormones improve your overall mood, and this improved mood further improves your overall perception of yourself.

Oh, also, since you are burning calories when you are physically active, you will improve the overall size and shape of your body if that is what you truly desire.

Here are simple things to do to become more physically active:

✓ Sit down one evening and begin to look at your routine after school.

✓ See if there is some free time between coming home from school, completing a few chores, and dinner.

✓ Then, insert walking into this small timeframe.

✓ Then, each evening, when this time comes, take your stopwatch, set it, and begin taking that walk for the time you have designated for the walk.

Do this consistently and if you ever feel the need to increase the time you designate to walking, do that. What you will find is that there will be a very big shift in how you feel after the walk vs. how you felt before. Also, there will be a huge difference in your body a few months later to what you were previously.

Now, most of the above will also work to improve your mental health, but there are other ways in which you can improve your mental health with activities explicitly aimed at improving your mental well-being.

How to Improve Your Mental Health

- **Read More**

Reading is one of those activities that not many of us have in our teens because, as mentioned, we are often under pressure to live up to the 'boys will be boys' moniker. So, we tend to lean more into activities that perhaps give us more adrenaline rush, even if that is not what we want.

Yet, reading, especially reading a piece of work that makes you lose yourself in it, reduces the level of stress that you are experiencing. The book transports you into a different world, where you can find characters and other people that you relate with, and this can make you feel better about yourself or simply make you laugh.

But maybe you are already a voracious reader, yet you are still struggling with your mental health. In that case, then, I ask you to change the types of books you are reading.

If you are often reading, let's say, history books or autobiographies, change and begin reading more plot-based books, like fiction or comic books. You will be pleased to learn that some of our favorite superheroes struggled with who they were before they became the superheroes that they are.

Such stories can give you a minor boost in how you feel, even if it is for a brief moment.

Additionally, reading makes you more knowledgeable, enhances your critical thinking, and boosts your creativity; all these combine to make you a little smarter than yesterday, and feeling smart improves your overall self-perception and, thus, your mental health, too.

- **Seek to Surround Yourself with Positivity**

Whether it is in media, or role models around you, surrounding yourself with positivity can greatly help in improving your mental health.

There is not much that you can do about societal pressure around you, but you can change the media that you consume to better represent who you are and who you want to be.

While many of the mainstream movies will often display a narrow, often unrealistic portrayal of what masculinity is, you can choose not to engage with this media and instead find media that portray masculinity in ways that you can relate to.

There are many media out here that you can relate to about what it means to be a man.

Good Will Hunting is one of my favorite movies of all time and that is because it is a movie that shaped and continues to shape my view on what it means to believe in myself and be a man. This is an old movie, but it has a timeless lesson on masculinity, self-esteem, and accepting yourself in order to live to your fullest potential.

This film is a heartfelt drama about Will Hunting, a young man who is a Math genius, but because he lacks the drive and desire for self-improvement, he ends up simply drifting through life. However, he soon finds it in him to unleash his full potential when he gets linked to a therapist, Dr. Sean

Maguire. Dr Sean challenges Will, helping him overcome his defeatist thoughts and improving his confidence.

Or, perhaps you don't like drama but would like to watch a movie on positive masculinity in an action-adventure. If so, then the *Lord of the Rings* series is for you. These thrilling adventure fantasy series explore themes of bravery, loyalty, and friendship among men, especially men who have odds stacked against them, men who were once boys like you - struggling with self-esteem and finding their place.

Alternatively, you can also try to find men who embody the traits that you want to embody and try to emulate them. These positive experiences will make you feel better about yourself and improve your overall mental health while also helping you find yourself through people you relate well with.

Our physical and mental health are closely linked to how we then perceive ourselves, which influences our self-esteem and confidence in who we are. Through practicing acceptance of who you are and working to improve your general body health rather than simply trying to appear as you think boys should appear, you will become much more in love with your body and, thus, minimize body image issues that result in low self-esteem.

Additionally, when you improve your mental health, either by reading or engaging in positive portrayals of masculinity away from the traditional view, you set yourself up for a very positive experience through your teenage years.

Once you have developed a positive body image, the next step you want to do is to build relationships with people who provide you with the support you need to continue in your journey towards becoming more confident.

Chapter 6: Building Healthy Friendships – How to Create a Strong Support System with Your Peers

I know what you are thinking as you read this headline.

'How can I build healthy relationships when I cannot even bring myself to be who I am in front of the people that I want to get close to? It's already hard for me to build relationships.'

I understand that, and in fact, I will not sit here and tell you that it has gotten any easier to make friends now that I am an adult. The levels of extreme self-consciousness that you display will often mean that you tend not to reveal too much about yourself for fear of pushing others away because of what you will reveal.

But I want you to view this chapter not as a strict guide on how to build friendships but rather as a guide on how to carry yourself in ways that will get other people to care about you, even without seeming like you are trying too much. This chapter is less about how to go out there and talk to people and more about *how to carry yourself in ways that other people get drawn to you.*

A problem I realized I had during my teens was that I often thought that I needed to have what I was going to say all planned out, including the right words to say at what point and how to say them just right. Because I was not confident in who I was, I felt as though this was the way to get some control of myself and maybe hold a conversation.

But this often failed spectacularly, you know why? Because I frequently came off as inauthentic. My classmates and other students often could read through it. In fact, at one point, one boy whom I was talking to in hopes that we could become friends looked me dead in the eye and asked,

"Why are you speaking like that? Like you are in theatre."

That was when the bubble burst!

Rather than let the conversation naturally take its course, I would try to force it into a given direction because that was what I thought people did. This made it very hard for me to build genuine relationships.

Another thing that made it very hard for me to build genuine relationships was simply the fact that I did not let myself become vulnerable to others. This point circles back to the repeated messaging of us not needing to show or speak about our emotions as boys.

So, as a teen boy, what marked my 'friendships,' if I may even call them that, was video games, sports, and maybe even girls. We never ever breached that barrier against vulnerability, and thus, the friendships often never developed into anything more substantial.

So, we often were in this situation where we are friends for years but never share any intimate emotional moments, are never vulnerable with each other and thus, never truly bond beyond the superficial level.

This then meant that I could never truly be myself around these boys, and so I needed a façade to fit in with them, and as you are aware by now, the façade of course, made me even feel more alienated.

Maybe you, too, have friends with whom you are never truly vulnerable; you perhaps never ask your crush out because you are afraid of getting to the point of being vulnerable. This is because you don't want the risk that comes with emotional vulnerability. You don't want to be 'found out' as sensitive.

Yet, one thing that I have learned in my life is that healthy relationships can be great places to build your self-confidence and esteem. They can be places where you simultaneously find comfort in being yourself while also being challenged to be a better person while remaining true to yourself.

How Healthy Relationships Build You

I still see the skepticism in your eyes. Perhaps you might be rolling them and thinking, *"Right! The old 'don't be friends with certain people' advice. I have heard it before."*

But not in the way I will present it to you. Sometimes, it's never about the advice but the perspective, and I am here to give you perspective rather than straight up.

Healthy relationships build you in many ways, including:

- **Provide You with Encouragement and Support**

No, I don't mean that your friends and family become your therapists on whom you dump all your feelings and emotions. Rather, having people who are genuinely interested in who you are, what you do, and what you think about **helps bring you out of your shell naturally.**

This is what happened to me, though it was much later in my life. I started interacting with boys in my class who, without me knowing, were peeling back my layers like onions.

They started slowly, by asking me for help in class, then by helping me with class projects and other things even without me asking for help. At first, I was skeptical because what do you mean you care what I think? What do you mean you want to help me yet I didn't ask for help?

I thought that they were building up to a prank that would make the whole school laugh at me because that's just who I was – a laughing stock.

Yet, that prank never came. Without knowing it, I was slowly lowering my defenses, becoming a bit more emotionally open with them, and even sharing my fears and issues with my perception of myself.

They listened to me and didn't offer up any advice as much as they simply sat with me and helped me wherever they could and that was when I learned that the right people with me could quite literally change my life. And it can change yours, too!

So, yes, healthy relationships will make you more self-confident and improve your self-esteem.

- **Shared Interests Gives You People to Relate to**

So, these boys that I met in my senior year as I was about to leave high school? Turns out that they, just like me, enjoyed doing the same things that I did. They enjoyed simply sitting down and reading when they could. They also enjoyed watching movies other than action movies. One of them was actually into romance. They enjoyed the same sports that I did. It almost was godsent.

Finding out that these boys all shared some of my interests really put into perspective that there was space for me, for boys like us, to live and enjoy our lives as we saw fit.

The shared interest provided us with a common ground on which we could form a strong friendship and build each other up in ways that nobody else could understand or do. Sure, we are only talking about interests, but these interests provided a sense of validation that I had never had previously in my life.

This sense of validation, this connection, this feeling of belonging, helped me break out of my shell and begin to feel confident in who I was. The mask that I had previously worn was torn off.

This could also be true for you. When you find other people that you share interests with, they can provide you with a sense of validation and give you the connection which could be all that you may need to become confident.

Now, I know most boys probably are raised with traditional masculine views, and thus, it will be hard for you to find your people, but trust me when you take your time to understand yourself, you will easily be able to tell which of your peers are worth letting into your life and which ones aren't.

I can see that you are probably now nodding in agreement to this, and that makes me happy. But then, I also know that there is a question in there somewhere.

How do I build healthy relationships?

That's a good question. While many advice books on this issue will often quickly delve into telling you what to do or not do to build relationships, I will begin by telling you how to present yourself to others, and everything else will fall into place.

How to Present Yourself to Others

The fear of being judged and the consequent lack of belief in yourself is something that others feel in you long before you approach them.

Thus, they will often interact with you with this knowledge, which affects how they treat you. This then creates a self-fulfilling prophecy where you believe that they are judging you, and so this affects your actions, which in turn makes the others judge you even more.

The opposite of this – present yourself as you would like them to perceive you, and here is how you will do that:

- **Be Genuine**

I understand, trust me, I understand. You are only trying to fit in and just make friends because you believe that that is the only way to be accepted.

But here is the reality of the situation – while pretending to be someone you are not might earn you a place in the group, it is only a matter of time before you either feel exhausted from pretending and, thus, feel disconnected from the group, or are found out, leading to the group excluding you.

Either of these outcomes will only worsen the feelings of self-hatred and make you feel worse about yourself.

Try, instead, to interact with others as your true self or as the best version of your true self that you can present.

Many teenage boys often get lost in trying to fit in that they forget that, when you find true friends, they will accept you for who you are, whether you are perfect or not, your flaws and all.

Thus, through each interaction, always ensure that you try to present yourself in a genuine way. I know that if your authentic self doesn't match the traditional view of masculinity, this can lead to ridicule, but I want you to do it anyway.

This presentation means that people will reject you, no doubt, but it also means that those who get close to you and become your friends will be people who genuinely want to be with you and be associated with you.

I mean, which is better – pretending to be someone you are not and hanging out with people you don't enjoy being with just so you can be part of the group, or presenting your authentic self to the world, getting rejected by some, but being accepted as you are by others?

Surely, the second option sounds better because it means that you now have a solid foundation to build genuine relationships and friendships.

- **Begin By Being a Listener**

Here is a connection between not listening and lacking self-confidence – being extremely self-conscious means that you spend much of the conversation with someone obsessing over how you look, speak, and what you will say in response.

This obsession means that you often never listen to what they are saying. So, when you inevitably have to answer to a detail that you weren't paying attention to, your inability to answer will make you feel embarrassed, further lowering your self-esteem.

So, I would urge you, instead, to simply stop and begin to listen. Listening and paying attention to what the other person is saying **builds trust and helps quickly establish rapport**. When you show the other person that you care enough about what they are saying, **they will, in**

turn, also pay attention to you. And when someone else pays keen attention to you, it does wonders for your esteem.

But how do you become a good listener? Here are some tips:

1. ***Try to Hold Eye Contact***: Oh, trust me, I know just how difficult it can be to look into someone's eyes when you already have high self-consciousness, but this is a great way to begin to listen better. Maybe you can start by looking at the other person for a short while, then looking away, perhaps at their hair. Ideally, you should make eye contact for about three seconds before looking away and looking back again. You can practice this on people you already trust, like your family and once you are comfortable doing it, then you can begin to do it on your peers in school.

2. ***Minimize Distractions***: Usually, as a self-conscious person, there is always something to distract you as someone else is talking to you. Whether it is a pen to fidget with, or your phone, or perhaps even playing with your clothing; fidgeting with these things helps ease some anxiety as we speak to the other person, but they also distract us from fully following the conversation. Thus, try as much as possible to limit the amount of distractions

when speaking to someone else. For example, keep your phone in your pocket or put the pen down. If you can't help but twiddle your finger because you feel nervous, then interlock your fingers, and you will feel much calmer; at least, that's what works for me.

3. ***Nod Along as They Speak or Show that You are Listening Through Short Interjections****:* When the person is making a point, nodding not only shows them you are listening, but it also makes you aware of the fact that they are speaking about something. This then means that you continue to pay close attention to them because you don't want to nod at inappropriate times. Alternatively, you can also give short interjections such as saying 'I see' or 'right' as they speak, which not only shows you are listening but also works to make you listen.

Becoming a good listener is a great way to win over people because we all want to be heard, and when you give someone a chance to be heard, they remember you. We tend to get so obsessed with wanting to be heard that we forget that we also need to listen so that we can then be heard when it is our time. Thus, listen first, and you will be heard.

Of course, becoming a good listener won't make you feel better about yourself instantly, nor will it make you friends quickly, but it will definitely draw people to you, and people being drawn to you will slowly begin to build your confidence.

- **Set Clear Boundaries**

While working to get people close to you, you must also be aware of the fact that you will need to set some boundaries. A good, healthy relationship, whether a friendship or romantic partnership, is founded on respect for each other, and this includes respect for each other's boundaries.

Now, you might be thinking that this could make your potential friends not want to hang out with you, but nothing could be further from the truth. Many teenage boys want to hang around other teenage boys who display confidence, and setting your boundaries firmly but respectfully, marks you as a confident person that the other boys will want to hang out with.

For example, I mentioned earlier that you might be uncomfortable skipping classes, and thus, when lacking confidence, you will follow the group, which would make you do this. However, when building healthy relationships, you make the other boys know early on that this is not something that you would want to do, but you do it in a way that doesn't make them look bad.

"Hey guys, I know we will be doing a lot of different stuff, but I just want to let you know that skipping class will not be part of that agenda."

This lets them know that you are open to having fun with them but that you won't skip classes for the fun. Even when they don't agree with you, if they are friends worth keeping around, they will respect that. If they don't, then consider that a sign that you should not pursue the friendship further.

Setting boundaries most likely won't make you the most popular kid in class or school, but I want you to know that being popular without having done the internal work to feel better about yourself will not make you feel better. If anything, it will only cast you into the spotlight and make you even more scrutinized than you thought you previously were.

- **Focus on Quality over Quantity**

Okay, I get it.

Like every teenage boy, you want to become popular, be the student whom every other student greets when they walk down the hallway, the student whom even teachers have some sense of admiration for.

But a question that one of my mentors asked when I told him that this is what I wanted was: *Okay, after all that, then what? After every student knows your name, then what?*

This was a question that I had never pondered, and as I sat there trying to answer it, I realized just how empty and shallow wanting to be popular just for the sake of it was.

Did that mean I had a lot of friends? Maybe, but it also meant that there were a lot more people who simply would want to hang around me just to be seen with the popular kids.

"When you become popular and haven't built genuine friendships, it's going to be hard to do that with your new status. Not impossible, but harder." My mentor said about my dreams of popularity.

As someone who is struggling with their identity and confidence, it is easy to get caught up in the imagination that having a lot of friends or being well-known will work wonders for your self-esteem, but trust me; it won't. It might make you feel better for a short while, but ultimately, you will have to be alone with yourself, and then, that's when it will hit you that you feel no better now that you are popular than you did when you weren't.

Instead, focus more on building a close-knit circle of friends whom you can form *a genuine emotional attachment to*, and that will *significantly improve your sense of self-worth.* The old adage of having a social circle to thrive often doesn't mention that the circle needs to be quality over quantity.

Look to build genuine friendships, not just have many 'friends' if you want to improve your self-confidence.

Building healthy friendships and romantic relationships will help you feel more confident in who you are because they will provide you with a support system for your mental and emotional needs. Even when you are not fully confident in yourself, when you have the right friends around you, then you will never be crippled with self-doubt and low self-confidence again because there will be people around you to hold you up and help put things into perspective, thus keeping you in line.

In addition to healthy friendships being key in building your confidence, so too is having a great relationship with your parents and other adults around you.

Chapter 7: Adults Dynamics – How to Navigate This Journey with Parents and Teachers

First, I won't deny the inescapable truth – sometimes, parents, teachers, or any other adult with authority around you might be the cause of your self-esteem issues.

Perhaps your parents are always criticizing you for even the smallest things. Maybe you forgot to do the dishes once, but then, it became a lecture on how you are irresponsible and cannot do simple things.

Or perhaps you feel as though they are not emotionally present at all. You feel as though they are not there to provide you with the guidance you need as you navigate these changes you are experiencing.

Maybe you have never been emotionally close to your father and, thus, cannot open up to him about these self-esteem issues you are facing, and it seems that the only times you get his attention is when you get into trouble or when talking about school.

And so, you begin to get into trouble to get their attention which spirals into a breakdown in the relationship, which further strips you of any small confidence you may have had.

At school, your teachers are unable to give you the guidance you need because perhaps they are also overwhelmed by having to deal with the other teenagers.

So, there you are, with no adult guiding hand to hold you and help you navigate this turbulence of emotions. You have to figure things out by yourself, and it is all driving you crazy.

So, I understand why you might be skeptical that you can navigate your teenage years with good adult guidance, but I want you to know it is very much possible for you to build a good, strong connection with adults, starting with your parents.

How to Navigate Family Dynamics

As much as we often want to get away from our families for one reason or another, the truth is that we will never truly get away from our families, and thus, we need to find ways in which we can deal with the issues at hand.

Now, I will not put the burden of responsibility of mending any broken relationship with your parents in your hands. Instead, I want to teach you how to take charge of the things within your control.

Conflict between your parent and you is inevitable, and thus, you can approach the conflict in ways that, rather than make things worse, could work to de-escalate the situation.

Here are some ways to do that:

- **Communicate Your Needs and Feelings Honestly and Respectfully**

Look, I know adults can be hard to deal with but hear me out.

This is perhaps the most challenging part, but you will need to learn how to communicate how you feel openly and respectfully with your parents or guardians.

Once again, it is difficult for you to express your opinion because you have been raised to believe that boys should just suck it in and deal with it internally, but the reason that you are here is that this way of living has been making you feel bad and you want to change it.

That inability to communicate how you feel means that you do not have any close relationships with people that you want to be close to. It also means that you have been unable to deal with certain personal issues and are having a hard time managing your emotions.

You'd rather avoid vulnerable issues than deal with them head-on, and all these compound into this self-deprecating sense of identity, where you simply want to just disappear from the world and not have to face any of the issues currently staring down at you.

But this book is here to guide you into becoming a better, more confident boy. To become more confident in yourself, you need to learn how to communicate your feelings with the adults.

Here is a guide on how you can get started:

1. **Be Respectful**: The first thing you want to do when expressing your opinion is to be respectful. I am sure you know that as a teenage boy you have a very small margin of error among many adults, and this might include even your parents or guardians. So, you want to be respectful when expressing your opinions, even if you feel frustrated or angry. Before expressing your sentiment, *take some*

time to calm yourself and rein in your impulses. Journaling and taking a walk before engaging in a difficult subject can help you calm down beforehand.

2. ***Avoid Accusatory Language***: You want to say how you feel without making the adult feel as though they are to blame for how you feel. Using the *"I statement"* usually works two-fold. First, it often makes you aware of how the world around you is impacting you, and this helps you become more self-aware and secondly, it minimizes defensiveness on the part of the adult. Nobody wants to feel as though they are being accused during a conversation, so when you use "I," you let the adult know that you are not blaming them for what happened but rather for how you feel about it. For example, *'The reason I act out is that I feel as though you do not care for me'* instead of *'You don't care about me; that is why I act this way.'* The first sentence opens room for more dialogue, while the second simply opens room for a confrontation full of attacks (accusations) and defenses (defensiveness).

Once again, let me reiterate that I understand that most adults will often deal with you suspiciously right from the get-go, and this, coupled with your teen impulses, means that you always react first and then think later. But in this chapter, I ask you to give respectful and open communication a chance. You will be amazed at the difference that it will make.

Not only will this make your parent or guardian respect you because you are speaking openly to them, but it will also make you feel better about yourself because you are no longer trying to bottle in your emotions.

- **Make An Effort to Forster Connections**

I don't know how to explain it but I know that you experience it – there is this feeling of shame and embarrassment that we often have about our families in our teens that we can't tell why we feel it. This feeling means, then, that we try to dissociate from our family members as we seek company elsewhere.

This feeling of shame comes from that heightened self-consciousness we are experiencing, which then makes us feel as though we need to disconnect from our families because we can no longer relate to them and find them 'cringe.' Unfortunately, this disconnect can leave us feeling lonely and lost, especially when we also cannot find community among our peers.

Thus, I want you to begin to make an effort to build strong connections with your family members. You parents, siblings, grandparents and other relatives around. Trust me; you don't want to get through your teens without mending some of these relationships because once you are an adult, you will look back in regret, thinking, *'I thought my family was weird, but that wasn't even a big deal!'* and perhaps it will be too late.

So, take part in those family traditions when you can, go out and bond with your siblings, and learn more about them because, trust me, ***it becomes harder to bond with your siblings as adults***. Spend quality time with your loved ones when you can, and express gratitude to those people in your family who are offering you support through this time.

Doing this will help you feel a lot better about yourself, and you will build a strong sense of identity, which will give you an anchor even as you spread out your wings and try to find another identity outside your family. Your family identity doesn't need to be at odds with the new identity you seek.

But if your family members aren't the best, then the next step is critical.

- **Limit Contact With Toxic Adults**

You don't need to face every issue head on and sometimes, avoidance can be the best form of conflict resolution.

Maybe some of the adults in your life just refuse to see reason and go from being simply annoying to being toxic. You have tried to be respectful to them, shared your opinions openly, and even tried to see things from their point of view, but they still refuse to give you the respect that you deserve.

Perhaps they **continue to criticize you and put you down endlessly** even when you have made it clear that you are willing to listen to them if they speak to you respectfully. Or perhaps they **continually display a lack of respect for your boundaries and feelings**. They are **manipulative and controlling**, often trying to shift the blame on you even when it is clearly their fault.

Their continued presence around you is eating away at the gains of confidence that you have made, and you can feel the hands from the past darkness pulling you back into that period of crippling self-doubt and wavering self-belief.

First, let me tell you that any adult who behaves in the ways mentioned above is most likely someone who has never dealt with their self-esteem issues, and thus, their toxic behavior is often a way of them trying to put others down just so that they can feel better about themselves. You don't want this person around you.

In that case, then the best decision that you can make is to limit contact with this toxic adult and try to avoid dealing with them directly.

If this person is a parent or guardian, this makes it very challenging, but you can try several things. First, if you have both parents or more than one guardian, then *express how you feel to the less toxic one*. They can be a way for you to learn to express yourself clearly while also providing you with the support you might need.

If you only have one parent or guardian, then *open up to your trusted teacher about how you feel or perhaps talk to the guidance and counseling professional at school*. Let them know how hard it is for you to have conversations with or bond with the adults in your life. Maybe they can provide you with the guidance you need.

Sometimes, the reason you have self-esteem issues might have nothing to do with yourself but rather with the adults that are around you. So, if you figure that the adults in your life are toxic to you and might never come around to respect you no matter what you do, then do not hesitate to limit contact with them as much as possible.

Even if limiting that contact is simply going to bed early before they get home or spending more time on your hobbies or with your friends, you will feel better when you are in a less toxic environment surrounded by positive people.

Adults will often be people that you want to avoid as much as possible as a teenager, but the reality is that no matter how independent you might be, you still are under the care of adults in your life, whether they are your parents, guardians, or teachers.

They will always get on your nerves, they may never understand you the way you want to be understood, and some might even be harmful to you. However, when you know how to navigate the dynamics with adults, you will find yourself able to navigate even the most challenging of relationships with them with absolute confidence and self-belief.

Because here is something that you may not know – ***sometimes the best way to build confidence is to actually just face issues head-on***, and your brain will adapt from there. Therefore, by confronting any issues you might have with adults around you openly and respectfully, you build that sense of self-assurance within yourself to then continue down on this path.

So, do not be afraid to tackle issues with adults in your life head-on because that is the best way for you to build your confidence and self-esteem. And in tackling issues with adults, you also get round to dealing with rejection and criticism and you need to know how to handle that.

Chapter 8: How to Handle Rejection and Criticism – What to Do When Things Don't Go Your Way

Whether big or small; rejections and criticisms do hurt us.

I wish someone had told me when I was younger that things won't always go my way. That would have saved me a lot of trouble and time. Sometimes, things just won't happen the way I wanted them to, and that was okay.

It took me forever to learn this lesson, but I believe that you don't need to take as long as I did to realize this, which is why I am bringing this lesson here to you.

When suffering from a lack of confidence, rejection or criticism can often feel like a dagger to the heart.

Perhaps after all the lessons you learned in this book, you finally gathered the courage to speak to your crush and ask her out. Beaming with confidence, you approach her and hit her with your best bars.

But then, it feels as though the world is spinning, and you feel as though you can't breathe. Your eyes are blurry. The answer was no.

Or maybe you gathered the courage to say no to things you don't want to do that don't represent who you are. You said no to skipping class with friends or said no to anything that you felt did not truly match who you are. This would surely earn you the respect of your peers, right?

No, instead, you get ridiculed. They laugh at you and, indeed, begin to call you a coward, as you feared. Nobody wants to be friends with you because they think you are no fun. The worst thing happened, and you begin to wonder whether all this was worth it.

It is all worth it, and here is how to handle rejection and criticism without ruining your newfound confidence:

- **Understand That Rejection/Criticism is Often About the Other Person, Not You**

That feeling of doubt creeping in after getting rejected or criticized will often lead to an avalanche of negative emotions that can feel overwhelming.

You begin to question whether you truly need to be confident in yourself or if it would simply be better if you just slid back into your cave and went with the flow. Life wasn't better that way, but at least you weren't getting rejected by your peers.

But hold it right there.

See, often, we think of getting rejected or being criticized as a failing on our part when just a small shift in perspective does wonders in helping you cope with rejection. Often, when we get rejected, it usually has very little to do with us and more to do with the other person and **their desires, values, and needs at that time**.

Maybe your crush rejected you because she was already seeing someone or wasn't interested in dating at that time, or maybe you approached them on a bad day. Maybe the people criticizing you did so because they felt threatened.

The thing is, when you shift your perspective, you will realize that rejection will often not have anything to do with who you are as a person but rather **with the circumstances at that moment in time**, most of which you have no control over.

I mean, sure, sometimes a person might reject you because of who you are or because of something you have done, but even then, you shouldn't let that dent your confidence. Instead,

- **Allow Yourself to Feel the Pain**

You got rejected, and all you want to do is just crawl under a bed and hide from the world as you let those feelings of self-doubt consume you as you slowly crawl back into the shell that you have worked so hard to free yourself from if that stops you from feeling this pain of rejection.

I understand this instinct and you shouldn't be too hard on yourself if your very first thought after getting rejected is to want to get rid of these feelings of pain or to try and pretend as though you aren't feeling it.

But the thing about trying to pretend you aren't feeling the pain of rejection or criticism is that **the pain will find other ways to present itself**, and you don't want that. You don't want to bottle up that pain only for it to unleash itself at the most inopportune moments.

So, after the rejection, instead of trying to think, *'I shouldn't feel this hurt. I am supposed to be confident,'* **acknowledge it** like this: *'I am feeling this pain because it is a normal part of getting rejected.'*

Once you acknowledge the feeling, then you move on to **the next part of naming what you are feeling**. Are you feeling angry? Disappointed? Sad? Left out? A mixture of all these emotions?

It is often a lot easier to deal with our emotions when we can name them because then we can find ways to express them.

Speaking of expressing them, once you can name your emotions, the next step is to *find ways in which you can express them*. You see that journal that you picked up earlier as a way of self-discovery. It also comes in handy here when you want to put into words the emotions you are feeling.

Write down your emotions, why you feel them, and how this is affecting you. When you are honest and raw about these emotions, you will find that you cope better with the rejection than you would have if you had tried to bury those feelings of being hurt.

- **Lean on Your Support System**

Okay, I can feel you cringe because it is very embarrassing for you to speak openly to your loved ones about your feelings, especially after getting rejected because you are probably thinking, *'What would they think of me? They would think I am weak or a loser who can't be accepted?'*

But this way of thinking is very detrimental to you because it leaves you worse off than you started, chipping away at your confidence just as much as the pain of rejection would if you let it fester.

I think one of the worst things about rejection or criticism isn't just the pain of the rejection itself but ***the feelings of isolation that you often experience afterward***. After getting rejected, you often begin to feel as though nobody wants to be around you. You feel as though the universe is rejecting or criticizing you.

You go from being somewhat confident about who you are and your prospects to feeling as though the world is out to get you, and thus, to protect yourself from this, you need to stay away from everything and everyone.

But nothing could be further from the truth.

Instead, when you have friends, family, or even a teacher or mentor whom you have a very close relationship with, lean on them for support and ***let them guide you on how best to deal with these emotions*** that you are feeling after the rejection.

Even when they won't give you any professional help or any life-changing advice, when they sit down and just listen to you, give you a shoulder to lean on and cry on, and tell you *'everything is going to be okay,'* that will be worth it.

You will realize, at that point, that, in fact, the world isn't rejecting you, that the criticism isn't the world turning its back on you. Rather, it was only a single person or a small group of people because otherwise, you have support everywhere. And in that moment, **you will feel a sense of relief** course through your body, putting you at ease.

- **Lean in on Things That Give You a Boost in Esteem**

Whether it is a physical activity like reading, writing, or doing any other hobby that provides you with a sense of balance and confidence, leaning into things that we love doing when experiencing pain can **help us process these emotions and cope with them healthily.**

Our hobbies are a great place for us to cope with the stress of the world around us, and this means that you will find yourself actually handling rejection or criticism well when you can lean into them and let them carry you into this alternate world.

So, take that walk and enjoy the sights and sounds of nature, take that evening jog with your friend, do whatever you enjoy doing and you will realize that you can handle the pain you are experiencing.

However, note that you should *lean into your hobbies to help process the pain and cope with it better, not to try and run away from the pain*. Thus, as you lean in on your hobbies, ensure that you also aren't trying to pretend as though you are feeling better or aren't hurting.

Acknowledge the pain and hurt even as you engage in these activities, and then let your hobbies help you find some calm in the storm for you to think through the emotions within.

- **Find the Lesson**

One of the best philosophies that I ever learned in life was that it doesn't matter what happens; with the right attitude, everything can be a lesson. In fact, I would go ahead and say that negative experiences, such as rejection, will often offer some of the lessons in life that stick with us – if we choose to find the lesson in them.

'But how can I do that?' You may be asking. Well, the first thing you want to do is to ask yourself some constructive questions that help you reflect on the rejection and the events surrounding it. Such questions include:

✓ Is there anything I did wrong in my approach?

✓ What could I have done differently in my approach before the rejection?

✓ What did this rejection reveal to me about myself and the other person/people?

✓ How can I use this revelation to improve myself?

When you view the rejection as an opportunity for growth, you will find that there are many different angles that you can take, which can help dig you down the path of deep introspection, from which you emerge on the other side wise, bolder, smarter and a much more confident version of yourself.

- **Keep Moving Forward**

You will get rejected many times but does that mean that you stop trying? If you fell off a bike, would you completely stop trying to learn how to ride it?

Sometimes, the best way to handle rejection is often to simply take a break, process your emotions, find the lesson, change your strategy and try again, even if you don't try in the same place as before.

That person that you have been crushing on rejected you, and it hurts. But does that mean that you close yourself off from approaching someone else that you may also like? No. Process the emotions of the previous rejection, find the lessons from that, and then try again.

The people that you thought were your friends rejected you because you refused to compromise your beliefs? Well, does that mean you stop trying to make friends? No. You process the pain of getting rejected by the people you considered friends and learn the lessons from it, the biggest lesson here is that you should pick your friends first and foremost based on shared values and then keep trying.

But if I keep trying and failing, won't that make me feel even worse about myself?

As I said, you need to process your emotions, learn lessons from them, change your approach, and then try again. Yes, if you keep trying, using the strategy that got you rejected in the first place without working through the emotions, then you might experience more rejections, which will chip away at your confidence.

However, when each rejection becomes a lesson in improving yourself, then it will only be a matter of time before that rejection becomes a yes, and then you will be glad that you believed in yourself even when it would have been easier to throw your hands up in defeat.

Rejection is a part of life, and as a teenage boy, it might seem as though it is the end of the world, especially if you are already struggling with self-acceptance and self-belief. However, rejection can also be a great platform on which you can build that unshakeable confidence you envy in others.

Do not go through your high school years in fear of rejection. Rather, I urge you to embrace the reality that rejection will be a part of life, prepare adequately, reflect consistently, and take rejection gracefully. In no time, you will be feeling confident with each acceptance that you get because you know what it takes to get you there.

Conclusion

These teenage years of your life will often make you feel as though you might be stuck in this life, in this cycle forever, and that nothing you do will ever come good or be of any worth.

With you having a hard time making friends, not being confident enough in yourself to even make small talk with your crush, can't even bring yourself to answer questions in class even when you are confident in your answer, you feel as though you just want to crawl into a hole.

But with the right approach, the right guidance, and an upbeat attitude, your teenage years can go from being filled with misery because you lack belief in yourself to an eye-opening time of your life that you will look back at fondly. And I know you want to change things, and that is why you bought this book.

Thus, I hope the lessons in this book provide you with the guidance that you need to let go of the shackles of lacking self-esteem and extreme self-consciousness and embrace the vast new world of self-belief and confidence.

Go crash it because I know you can!

www.ingramcontent.com/pod-product-compliance
Lightning Source LLC
LaVergne TN
LVHW041230080426
835508LV00011B/1135